Contents

Words appearing in the text in bold, **like this**, are explained in the Glossary.

Witnesses to the Holocaust

Between 1941 and 1945, thousands of men, women and children were **transported** from eastern Europe to a place called Auschwitz-Birkenau, in Poland. They travelled for many days by train in over-crowded cattle trucks with very little water and even less food. Upon arrival, as the wide truck doors were slid back, they were greeted by the sight of guards with guns, whips and dogs. Able-bodied men, women and older children were separated out to swell the ranks of forced-labour gangs or to become human guinea pigs for medical experimentation. The sick, elderly and women with small children and babies were marched immediately to specially built **gas chambers** where they were murdered.

All were victims of the Holocaust. This was the planned and systematic murder of well over six million people carried out on the orders of Adolf Hitler by the **Nazis**, mainly between 1940 and 1945. The vast majority – nine in every ten – were **Jews**, but **Gypsies**, **Jehovah's Witnesses**, the mentally and physically handicapped, **homosexuals** and **Slavs** were also amongst this unimaginably vast number.

Unable to Work

Prisoners who arrived at Auschwitz were separated into those fit for hard labour and those too young, old or weak to work. This painting by David Olère, called *Unable to Work* (1945), captures the sad image of those too weak, old or young to work being sent to their deaths in the gas chambers.

Art, Music and Writings from the Holocaust

Susan Willoughby

Heinemann

www.heinemann.co.uk/library

Visit our website to find out more infor[mation about Heinemann Lib]rary books.

To order:
- ☎ Phone 44 (0) 1865 888066
- 📠 Send a fax to 44 (0) 1865 314091
- 💻 Visit the Heinemann Bookshop at www[.heinemann.co.uk/library to b]rowse our catalogue and order online.

First published in Great Britain by Heinemann Library, Halley Court, Jordan Hill, Oxford, OX2 8EJ, part of Harcourt Education.
Heinemann is a registered trademark of Harcourt Education Ltd.

Editorial: Andrew Farrow and Dan Nunn
Design: David Poole and Tinstar Design Limited
    (www.tinstar.co.uk)
Illustrations by Martin Griffin
Picture Research: Maria Joannou and Thelma Gilbert
Production: Viv Hichens

Originated by Ambassador Litho Ltd
Printed in Hong Kong, China by
    Wing King Tong

ISBN 0 431 15370 1 (hardback)
07 06 05 04 03
10 9 8 7 6 5 4 3 2 1

ISBN 0 431 15375 2 (paperback)
07 06 05 04 03
10 9 8 7 6 5 4 3 2 1

British Library Cataloguing in Publication Data
Willoughby, Susan
    Art, Music and Writings from the Holocaust. -
    (The Holocaust) 1. Holocaust, Jewish (1939-
    1945) - Juvenile literature 2. World War, 1939-
    1945 - Art and the war - Juvenile literature 3.
    World War, 1939-1945 - Literature and the war
    - Juvenile literature 4. World War, 1939-
    1945 - Music and the war - Juvenile literature
    I. Title
    940.5'318

A full catalogue record for this book is available from the British Library.

Acknowledgements
The publishers would like to thank the following for permission to reproduce photographs: AKG London pp. **9**, **10**, **11**; Art Collection, Ghetto Fighters House Museum (Beit Lohamei Haghetaot Museum), Israel/Yair Pelieg pp. **19**, **49**; Beate Klarsfeld Foundation/David Olere pp. **4**, **5**, **13**, **38**; Deutsches Historishes Museum p. **15**; Florida Center for Instructional Technology/Dr Roy Winkelman pp. **36**, **37**; Hulton Getty Picture Collection p. **16**; Kurt Jiri Kotouc & Marie Rut Krizkova/George Brady pp. **43** (top), **43** (bottom); Mary Evans Picture Library p. **6**; Mervyn Peake p. **39**; Mezcenstwo Walka and Zaglada Zydow Polsce, courtesy of Florida Center for Instructional Technology pp. **28**, **29**; Narodni Filmovy Archiv p. **44**; Randall Bytwerk, CAS Department, Calvin College p. **12**; Scott Sakansky/Florida Center for Instructional Technology p. **40**; Terezín Memorial pp. **45**, **46**; Thomas Haas p. **47**; University Library, Jerusalem p. **24**; USHMM pp. **7**, **8**, **17**, **25**, **26**, **30**, **32**, **34**, **35**; Yad Vashem pp. **14**, **20**, **21**, **22**, **23**, **27**

The pictures on pages **22** and **23** are taken from the album *The Legend of Ghetto Lodz, 1940–44*, Gouache, ink and pencil on paper. (Jasny Collection, gift of Chara Jasny. Courtesy of the Yad Vashem Art Museum, Jerusalem.)

Cover photograph reproduced with the permission of Alexandre Olère.

The publishers would like to thank Jonathan Gorsky of the Council of Christians and Jews for his assistance in the preparation of this book.

Every effort has been made to contact copyright holders of any material reproduced in this book. Any omissions will be rectified in subsequent printings if notice is given to the publishers.

Disclaimer
All the Internet addresses (URLs) given in this book were valid at the time of going to press. However, due to the dynamic nature of the Internet, some addresses may have changed, or sites may have ceased to exist since publication. While the author and publishers regret any inconvenience this may cause readers, no responsibility for any such changes can be accepted by either the author or the publishers.

Terrible scenes

After he was liberated, David Olère painted some of the terrible scenes that he had witnessed and kept in his memory, including this one. Unlike many Jews, David survived because the Nazis made use of his artistic talents.

Auschwitz evidence

Auschwitz-Birkenau was just one of six **death camps** created to carry out Hitler's '**Final Solution**' – the complete extermination of Jews and other **undesirables**. Yet Auschwitz is the one that has come to symbolize the Holocaust. This may be because so many people – 1.25 million – lost their lives there and the camp remains as evidence of the terrible things that happened there. We also have many spoken and written records from survivors of Auschwitz, and the experiences of those who died are captured in the work of artists, poets and writers.

David Olère – artist of death

David Olère was born in Warsaw, Poland in 1902. He was an artist from an early age. He was working in France as a professional artist when the Nazis invaded in 1939. Along with thousands of French Jews, he was eventually arrested and transported to Auschwitz-Birkenau in February 1943. There he became a *Sonderkommando*, a member of a special work force that was made to empty the gas chambers and transport the bodies to the **crematoria** for burning. Normally, this work force was changed every three or four months and the men were sent to the gas chambers themselves. Unlike most of the others, he survived. He was saved from death by his artistic ability. He drew and illustrated postcards for the Nazi officers and translated radio broadcasts. David's work is very important because there are no photographs of what happened in the gas chambers.

What was the Holocaust?

To understand how the Holocaust came about we must go back to 1933 when Adolf Hitler and the Nazi Party came to power in Germany. Germany had been defeated in the First World War, which ended in 1918. Then, between 1918 and 1933, Germany became a **democracy** known as the Weimar Republic. However, the country's parliament failed to bring about economic recovery in Germany and, by 1932, the country was in the grip of a deep **depression**. Over 6 million people were unemployed. It was a desperate situation that opened the way for extremists to come to power.

The rise of Adolf Hitler and the Nazis

Adolf Hitler claimed to have the answers to Germany's problems. The German people were won over by his confident promises of **prosperity**. He raised their spirits by telling them that they were members of a 'master race' that would soon rule the world. He told them that their armies had been betrayed into surrendering at the end of the First World War. People voted for his Nazi Party in the **Reichstag** elections of 1932 and Hitler became Chancellor (a kind of Prime Minister) in 1933. By 1934, he had been given the power to become a **dictator**.

A pure race

Hitler said that this German master race must be made up of pure **Aryans**. He believed that the Aryan race was superior to all other races, and that it must be kept pure at all costs. Hitler knew that **anti-Semitism** was common in post-war Germany, so when he blamed the Jews for Germany's troubles, people believed him.

Adolf Hitler

Hitler was born in Austria, in 1889. After the First World War, he became involved in politics. In 1925, his book, *Mein Kampf*, was published. In it he wrote about his belief in the superiority of the Aryan race and the inferiority of Jews.

Euthanasia

From 1940, the Nazis carried out a **euthanasia programme** to kill off handicapped children and adults. They were seen as a threat to the strength and purity of Germany and had to be 'removed'. This was the beginning of mass murder using gas or lethal injections. It gave the Nazis the idea for how the '**Final Solution**' could be carried out. Hartheim Castle in Austria (seen here) was one of the killing centres.

Of course, not all Germans supported Hitler. Many lost their lives for criticizing him and for attempting to end his cruel regime. Many others opposed him but were too afraid to criticize him openly.

While the Jews felt the full force of Hitler's racism, others also suffered. Jehovah's witnesses, homosexuals, the mentally and physically handicapped, Gypsies and, later, the Slav people of eastern Europe, all became victims of Nazi persecution.

Persecution, discrimination and slaughter

In the years between 1933 and 1939, Jews in Germany were persecuted, deprived of their property and their rights, sent to **concentration camps**, beaten and murdered. Children suffered as they were expelled from their schools, separated from their friends and often their own families.

As Hitler's armies moved across Europe after 1939, Jews were rounded up and put into camps. In eastern Europe, mobile killing squads – the **Einsatzgruppen** – wiped out thousands of Jews, Gypsies and other 'undesirables' in mass executions. Jews were forced to enter **ghettos**. There they lived in filth, squalor and daily terror of **transportation**. Most of those people transported were never seen again, as the Nazis carried out their 'Final Solution'.

Artistic responses

These terrifying experiences produced an amazing outpouring of art, poetry and writing. Many found that they could only express their feelings of pain, bewilderment and loss through poetry, painting, drawing or writing. Many used their talents deliberately to make sure that they left behind a record of the things that the Nazis had done. This was the only way that they could protest.

The culture of Nazism

Even during the difficult days after the First World War, Berlin was regarded as one of the cultural centres of Europe. It was renowned for its scholars, art collections and music. However, when the **Nazis** came to power they banned the work of some writers, musicians and artists whose work they considered to be '**degenerate**'. On the other hand, Hitler wanted to maintain the impression that Germans enjoyed a rich cultural life. This was part of his **propaganda** programme, as was the art, music and writing that he approved.

'Degenerate' culture

In Berlin today, in the square in front of the Opera, an unusual memorial can be found. It consists of a pane of glass set in the ground. Looking down into the depths beneath, only empty bookshelves can be seen. Beside it is a plaque, which reads: 'Wherever books are burnt, men will eventually be burnt.'

The memorial marks the place where, on 10 May 1933, thousands of books were publicly burned. As they were thrown into the fire by Stormtroopers (the Nazi Party's private army, also known as the 'Brown shirts') and pro-Nazi students, the names of the undesirable authors were read out. It was like an execution. For many, it must have been an alarming sight as books by respected scholars and writers such as Albert Einstein, Sigmund Freud, Ernest Hemingway and Sinclair Lewis went up in flames. They were declared undesirable either because their authors were **Jewish** or because they promoted ideas and lifestyles of which the Nazis disapproved. They were described as 'degenerate'. At midnight, Joseph Goebbels (Hitler's 'Minister of Propaganda and Public Enlightenment') arrived at the scene and delivered a stirring speech hailing the dawn of a new era. But what kind of era would it be?

Bertold Brecht – a 'degenerate' playwright

Bertold Brecht was a playwright who openly criticized Hitler. His work was banned and he escaped from Germany in 1933. He returned in 1948 and became recognized as one of Germany's greatest writers.

Acceptable literature

Around 2500 writers left Germany in the early years of Nazi rule, in order to be free to write as they pleased. Writers who supported, and who were supported by, the Nazis, replaced them. To the outside world, German literature seemed to be flourishing. Joseph Goebbels' Ministry of Propaganda supervised Germany's 2500 publishing houses, 6000 state libraries and 23,000 bookshops. Three thousand authors made sure that Germans read what the Nazis wanted them to read in the 20,000 books that were published annually. There were fifty prizes awarded each year to reward them for their loyal efforts. However, Hitler's own book, *Mein Kampf* (which translates into English as 'My Struggle'), remained the best seller. He wrote this while he was in prison in 1923. In it he set out his ideas about the superiority of the **Aryan** race. By 1940, six million copies had been sold!

The theatre

A similar fate was suffered by playwrights and actors. Many plays were banned and half of Germany's actors found themselves out of work. Instead, theatres were used to stage large-scale productions glorifying Germany. People were encouraged to go to the theatre with cheap or even half-price tickets, which could be used to see ten plays. However, they were not allowed to choose the play, the date or the place!

The sight of such mass audiences convinced many people in Europe that some kind of cultural revolution was underway in Germany. Shakespeare's plays continued to be performed, particularly *The Merchant of Venice*. This particular play appealed to the Nazis because the character of the Jewish merchant, Shylock, matched the evil and greedy image of a Jew that the Nazis wanted to portray. However, the Nazis still changed the story so that the marriage of Jessica (Shylock's daughter) to Lorenzo, a Christian, was made acceptable to Nazi race laws. They did this by suggesting that Shylock was not really her father!

'Degenerate' art and music

It was not only books that the **Nazis** destroyed. In 1939, 4000 paintings, including masterpieces by Paul Cézanne, Pablo Picasso, Vincent Van Gogh, Henri Matisse and Paul Gaugin, were publicly burned. They had been part of an exhibition of '**degenerate**' art in Munich in 1937. It had attracted two million visitors. The Nazis had hoped that they would respond with the same angry reaction as the visitor quoted here:

'The artists ought to be tied up next to their pictures so that every German can spit in their faces – but not only the artists, also the museum directors who, at a time of mass unemployment, poured vast sums into the ever open jaws of the perpetrators of these atrocities.'

Hitler disliked all forms of modern art but the work of some artists was also banned because they were **Jewish** or Russian. To him, all Russians were **communists** and **Slavs**. Hitler despised both. For example, the work of the Russian-born artist, Wassily Kandinsky, was banned. Even though he had been born in Russia, Kandinsky lived and worked in Germany. A similar fate befell the work of Marc Chagall. Chagall was born in Russia but spent most of his life in France. His family background was Jewish and this shows up in many of his paintings.

Marc Chagall – a 'degenerate' artist

This painting is called *The Soldier*. It shows the use of bright colour and irregular forms that are typical of Chagall's work. This made it unpopular with Hitler. He also didn't like the influence of Chagall's Russian-Jewish origins on the artist's paintings.

Nazi art

Hitler decided and dictated acceptable artistic styles himself. As a young man, he had studied art in Vienna. He had developed his own style of painting and had attempted, unsuccessfully, to become an artist. He rejected the vivid colours and irregular shapes of modern artists, insisting instead on the use of natural colours and realistic forms. Paintings that he approved of reflected his vision of the perfect German and idealized German life. German painters who produced these ideal works of art were well rewarded financially and looked after. Those who refused to produce art that was acceptable to the Nazis, and wished to remain free to express themselves, were forced to leave Germany or face a life of poverty.

'Degenerate' music

Hitler also had fixed ideas about music. By the 1930s, Germany, and especially the nightclubs of Berlin, had taken in the craze that swept the USA in the 1920s – jazz. Hitler disapproved of this partly because it was loud and brash, but also because it was associated with immorality and it was the music of the black Americans, who were members of an **inferior** race according to Nazi beliefs.

Other musicians and composers were also experimenting with new rhythms and sounds in the early 1930s. Hitler banned

The ideal Germans

This picture portrays the ideal of German country life. The family are shown bearing all the characteristics of Hitler's pure, **Aryan** Germans – fair hair, blue eyes and regular features.

this kind of 'modern' music. Several of the banned composers and musicians were also Jews. These included Arnold Schoenberg (composer), Otto Klemperer and Bruno Walter (conductors). They were forced to leave Germany and found refuge in the USA, Britain or elsewhere in Europe. Many Jewish musicians eventually perished in the **gas chambers** of the death camps.

Acceptable music

Hitler loved music that glorified Germany. His favourite composers were Richard Wagner and Ludwig van Beethoven. Richard Strauss and Carl Orff were employed to compose music for the Olympic Games in Berlin in 1936. Much of the music composed for the Nazis was marching music. Folk music and dancing were popular with the **Nazi Youth**, who also formed choirs and orchestras. Operettas and ballets were performed in Berlin throughout the war years.

Nazi culture and the Jews

Stolen treasures

Hitler built up a huge art collection for himself. It was his intention to make his birthplace, the town of Linz in northern Austria, the art capital of the world. As the German armies swept across Europe after 1939, art galleries were looted and the stolen treasures taken back to Germany. Both Hitler and Goebbels had huge private collections of stolen works of art worth millions of pounds.

Anti-Semitic art

This illustration from a children's book is called *The Experience of Hans and Else with a Strange Man*. The caption says, 'Here kids, I have some candy for you. But you both have to come with me.' It shows the Jew as a threat to Aryan children. It is deliberately designed to encourage children to fear and hate Jews.

Art as propaganda

Art played an important part in Hitler's **anti-Semitic propaganda**. While artists were ordered to paint beautiful portraits of **Aryan** Germans, they were required to show **Jews** as ugly and distasteful. The pictures were designed to encourage fear, suspicion and revulsion. Such images became part of everyday life. Children saw them in their schoolbooks. They appeared in newspapers such as *Der Stürmer* and on posters in public places. Through this kind of constant exposure, many Germans were persuaded to believe what Hitler was saying about the Jews.

Painting and playing to survive

While the **Nazis** 'cleansed' Europe of the art, music and writing of Jews, they were happy to make use of Jewish talents in the **concentration camps**. For many artists and musicians, this meant they could avoid hard labour and in some, though not all, cases survive. For example, David Olère (*see page 5*) survived because he wrote letters for Nazi officers and decorated them with flowers. He was also a scholar. He spoke six languages including English, French and Russian. This made him useful as a translator.

Dinah Gottlieb

Dinah Gottlieb was born in Czechoslovakia. Before the war, she studied graphics and sculpture. She was taken, with her mother, to the Terezin **ghetto** and from there in September 1943 to Auschwitz **death camp**. She was fortunate because, unlike most, her **transport** was not sent straight to the gas chambers.

At first she was made to work at hard labour, lifting heavy rocks. However, her artistic talent was noticed by one of the officers and she was given the task of painting the slogan '*Arbeit Macht Frei*' ('work liberates') on walls all over the camp. Soon her drawings were in demand by Nazi officers. She came to the attention of Joseph Mengele, the chief doctor of the camp and the man responsible for carrying out horrific medical experiments. She spent most of the remaining time in the camp drawing his victims on his orders. This was to help him with his research into inherited characteristics. When most of the other Czech inmates were sent to the gas chambers in 1944, Dinah and her mother were among a very small number who were spared. Dinah's artistic ability saved her life.

Playing to live

It is hard to imagine that among the starved, **emaciated** faces of the inmates of Auschwitz, Bergen-Belsen and other camps were some of Europe's most talented musicians. The Nazi officers took advantage of this. Camp orchestras were formed and were ordered to entertain them. Cruelly, they were also used to 'welcome' new arrivals to the camps as the cattle trucks carrying them drew into the sidings. At Auschwitz, the orchestra was ordered to play while naked women and children queued up to be herded into the **gas chambers**.

Painting to survive

David Olère drew this picture of himself shortly after his liberation from Auschwitz. It is called *For a Crust of Bread*. In it he shows himself writing and illustrating a letter for which he was rewarded with a crust of bread.

13

Persecution and rejection

As we have seen, when Hitler came to power, his attack on the **Jews** and other 'misfits' was swift. By 1935, most Jews were no longer free to own businesses, practise medicine, mix freely with non-Jewish Germans or marry them. Mixed marriages were declared unlawful and families were split up. Jewish children were humiliated in their schools. Their friendships with non-Jewish children were destroyed. Jews were also deprived of their German nationality – they became stateless people.

After 1938, large numbers of German and Austrian Jews attempted to find new and safer homes in other lands. Some were successful, but most were refused entry to countries like the USA, Britain and Canada, whose governments wanted to restrict **immigration**. Many of those who went to other European countries, such as Belgium and the Netherlands, were eventually imprisoned by the Nazis after 1939. Their sense of rejection and isolation is shown in paintings and writings of the time.

Felix Nussbaum (1904–44)

Felix was born in Osnabrück, Germany in 1904. The experience of his family is an example of the struggle to find a safe home shared by thousands of German Jewish families after 1933. Felix studied art in Berlin, where his paintings were exhibited. When Hitler came to power, Felix fled to Italy to escape **persecution**. His parents left Osnabrück in search of safety and joined their son in Italy. However, they soon felt homesick and returned to Germany. Felix then moved to Belgium, where he thought he could paint freely. After the German **occupation** of Belgium in 1940, he was arrested and sent to a camp at Saint Cyprien in southern France. He escaped and lived in hiding, but continued to paint. His powerful paintings show his fear for his people and his feelings of isolation and persecution. Finally, Felix, his wife and son were arrested and sent to Auschwitz, where they died in August 1944. His paintings survived because they were left behind when he was **transported** to Auschwitz.

No place of refuge

In this painting, Felix Nussbaum captures the fear and despair of a Jewish refugee. He has no place of refuge anywhere in the world, symbolized by the globe. He is in a narrow, bare, prison-like room. His only possessions are in a small bundle at his side. This is one of a number of his pictures that tell the story of the Jewish people and their sufferings.

Threesome

Felix Nussbaum painted this picture of himself, his wife Felka and his son Jaqui in hiding in January 1944. This was one of his last pictures. In it he tries to capture the plight of Jews, quietly enduring persecution, afraid but still hopeful.

Refugee Blues

The mood of Felix Nussbaum's painting of the refugee on page 14 is reflected in the words of a poem called *Refugee Blues* by the English poet, W. H. Auden, written in March 1939. Auden was living in Berlin at the time when Hitler rose to power. He left Europe for America in 1939.

> *Say this city has ten million souls,*
> *Some are living in mansions, some are living in holes:*
> *Yet there's no place for us, my dear, yet there's no place for us.*
>
> *Once we had a country and we thought it fair,*
> *Look in the atlas and you'll find it there:*
> *We cannot go there now, my dear, we cannot go there now...*
>
> *Thought I heard the thunder rumbling in the sky;*
> *It was Hitler over Europe, saying 'They must die':*
> *O we were in his mind, my dear, O we were in his mind.*
>
> *Saw a poodle in a jacket fastened with a pin,*
> *Saw a door opened and a cat let in:*
> *But they weren't German Jews, my dear, but they weren't German Jews...*
>
> *Stood on a great plain in the falling snow;*
> *Ten thousand soldiers marched to and fro:*
> *Looking for you and me, my dear, looking for you and me.*

Five verses from *Refugee Blues* by W. H. Auden

The diary of Anne Frank

Anne Frank was born in Frankfurt, Germany in 1929. Her father, Otto, took the family to Amsterdam in the Netherlands in 1933 to escape **Nazi persecution**. After the German invasion of the Netherlands in 1940, Anne's life changed. The **Jewish** family were forced to go into hiding to avoid arrest. During this time, Anne kept a diary. Her daily accounts of life in Amsterdam help us to see what it was like for young Jews living under Nazi rule. In 1944, the family was betrayed and their hiding place was raided by the Nazis. Anne was sent to Auschwitz and then to Bergen-Belsen where she died of **typhus**.

The voyage of the *St Louis*

In May 1939, the *St Louis* set sail from Hamburg carrying 960 Jewish passengers. They had bought tickets to carry them to Havana, Cuba and **visas** to gain entry. The voyage began with optimism and excitement. It ended in tragedy. When they arrived at Havana, they were refused entry. Among them were many children including thirteen-year-old Liesel Joseph, who has left behind her image of life on board the ship during this difficult time. Eventually, a small number were allowed to land. The ship was then forced to return to Europe. Those who were allowed to land in France, Belgium and the Netherlands were put in camps. Very few of the passengers survived the Holocaust.

An extract from Anne Frank's diary

Saturday, 20 June 1942.
[Anne tells 'Kitty', her diary, the story of her life so far:]

'After May, 1940, good times rapidly fled: first the war, then the **capitulation**, followed by the arrival of the Germans. That was when the sufferings of us Jews really began. Anti-Jewish decrees followed each other in quick succession. Jews must wear a yellow star, Jews must hand in their bicycles, Jews are banned from trams and forbidden to drive. Jews are only allowed to do their shopping between three and five o'clock and then only in shops which bear the placard 'Jewish shop'. Jews must be indoors by eight o'clock and cannot even sit in their gardens after that hour... Jews may not visit Christians, Jews must go to Jewish schools, and many more restrictions.'

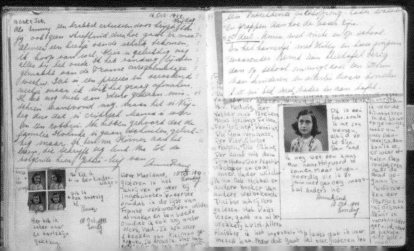

August 3th 1939

THE GERMAN SHIP „St. LOUIS" FROM; HABANA TO ANTW

Liesel Joseph
LONDON
11 years ENGL

On board the *St Louis*

Liesel Joseph was on board the *St Louis*. In her picture, the bright sky expresses her hope for the future. The dark and gloomy ship, without any signs of life on board, shows the anxiety and despair that must have overwhelmed the passengers.

The letters of Julius Hermann

Julius Hermann was another passenger on the *St Louis*. After the ship returned to Europe, he landed in France and was placed in an **internment camp** at Saint Cyprien, near the Spanish border – this was before the German invasion. In this extract from one of his letters to his relatives in the USA, he provides a very clear picture of his suffering:

'All the clothes, underwear and other articles of use that were to come with us have all been lost... You can imagine that the squalor that you see here makes the situation worse. Typhus and malaria, as well as lice, fleas, and tremendous hordes of flies, give you a sense of it. Sand is a foot deep, and we are dreading the coming storms which will blow the sand into the cracks of our temporary barracks... Rats and mice also seek refuge in our housing when the weather gets colder... These conditions are almost unbearable.

'When one read and heard earlier travel descriptions from prison camps, etc., about the conditions there, one viewed all this as impossible. Now, when one has to experience this oneself, the question needs to be posed, how can this happen in the 20th century?'

Julius was deported to Auschwitz in August 1942, where he died. His wife, daughter and other relatives, from whom he had been separated since 1935, were sent to the Riga **ghetto** (in Latvia) where they too almost certainly died.

Images of ghetto life

As Hitler's invading armies occupied the countries of eastern Europe, the **Nazis** dealt ruthlessly with the large **Jewish** populations. They were either wiped out in mass killings by the ***Einsatzgruppen*** or they were forced to live in **ghettos** – areas of cities or towns that were eventually walled or fenced off to separate Jews and others, including **Gypsies**, from the rest of the population. There were 356 ghettos in Eastern Europe. They became overcrowded, dirty and unhealthy places. Violence and cruelty were parts of everyday life and the people lived in constant fear of death or **deportation**. Perhaps one of the worst features was that the Nazis gave the responsibility for running the ghettos to a Jewish council. Jewish policemen ensured that the rules were kept.

A Jewish committee drew up the list of people to be deported. So it sometimes seemed that many of the terrible things that happened to Jews were carried out by Jews themselves. The bitterness that this caused is seen in some of the writings that came from the ghettos and camps. By 1945, only a small proportion of ghetto dwellers had survived to speak of their experiences. However, the diaries, poetry and vivid pictures and paintings of those who vanished leave us with a deeper insight into the reality of life in the ghettos. They also show us very clearly that people managed to maintain an amazingly rich cultural life in the face of such hardship.

Jewish ghettos

This map shows the locations of the main Jewish ghettos in Nazi occupied Europe, 1941–42.

The entrance to the Lodz ghetto

This painting, by an artist in the Lodz ghetto in Poland, shows Jews arriving with their belongings at the entrance to the ghetto.

Isaac Katzenelson

Isaac Katzenelson was born in the former Soviet Union in 1886 but grew up in Warsaw, Poland. When Hitler began to send Polish Jews to the ghettos and camps, he escaped to France. He was arrested and put in a **concentration camp** at Vittel. From there he was deported to Auschwitz where he died. His poem has since been set to music:

*I looked out of the window and beheld the
    hands that struck;
Observed who did the beating up, and who
    were beaten up;
And wrung my hands for very shame... oh
    mockery and shame:
It was by Jews, alas, by Jews my Jewish folk
    was slain!...*

*They tore the doors down, tore inside with
    curses and commands;
Invaded Jewish homes with clubs held ready
    in their hands;
Found us and beat us, bullied us to where the
    wagons stood –
Both young and old! And soiled the light of day,
    and spat at God...*

*The German stands apart, as if he's laughing
    at the scene –
The German keeps his distance – has no need
    to come between;
Ah, woe is me! He's managed it! By Jews my
    Jews are slain!
Behold the wagons! Ah, behold the agony, the
    shame.*

Three verses from *The Song of the Slaughtered Jewish People* by Isaac Katzenelson

The Lodz ghetto

The two largest ghettos in eastern Europe were in Poland – Warsaw, the biggest, and then Lodz. Lodz was the last ghetto to be destroyed. Its inmates left behind a vast amount of information about what had happened during their time there. Much of this was in the form of paintings, diaries and poetry. The Lodz ghetto was surrounded by a wooden fence and barbed wire. Once inside, Jews were not allowed to leave on penalty of death. German soldiers guarded the outside, Jewish ghetto police guarded the inside.

As time went by, the inmates became exhausted by hard labour and weak from hunger and disease. Of the 233,000 who entered the ghetto in 1939, only 164,000 remained by May 1940. In spite of this, music, theatre, art, concerts and educational lectures were very much part of life in the ghetto. The inmates were determined to retain some dignity and quality of life in the face of degradation and humiliation. This also happened in most of the other ghetto communities, such as those at Kovno (in Lithuania), Warsaw (in Poland) and Terezín (near Prague in Czechoslovakia).

Music, writing and drama

Drama and songs did not just help people in the ghettos maintain some pride and quality of life. They also preserved their traditions, religion and culture. Study, writing and songs also helped people to deal with much of their despair, anger and frustration. Laughter played an important part, even though the humour was often bitter and sarcastic. Music was very important, too. Musicians and composers in the ghettos wrote new lyrics to old songs so that the inmates could sing out their defiance.

A concert party

It is hard to imagine that the happy, smiling faces of this group of actors, like others in the Lodz ghetto, lived in overcrowded and unhealthy conditions and in constant fear.

Photographs from the ghetto show street singers surrounded by children and adults. Artists portrayed musicians playing in coffee- and tea-houses where everyone joined in. Small orchestras or quartets performed regularly. Photographs and drawings also survive of ghetto productions with costumes and specially designed scenery. Creativity seems to have provided some compensation for the lack of food and the indignities that ghetto dwellers had to endure. Reading, writing and studying stimulated minds and kept alive the hope of a return to normality.

A song from the Warsaw ghetto

Let us be jolly and share good jokes
We'll yet sit shiva * when Hitler croaks.
Biri-bi, bam-bam-bam
(Repeat the chorus)
Let us take comfort, forget our sorrow;
Through Hitler's body the worms will burrow.
(Chorus)
Who drive us now to Treblinka's horror
Themselves will be under the ground tomorrow
(Chorus)
Arm in arm, we'll yet make merry
And dance through a German cemetery.

* To 'sit shiva' is a Jewish mourning ritual.

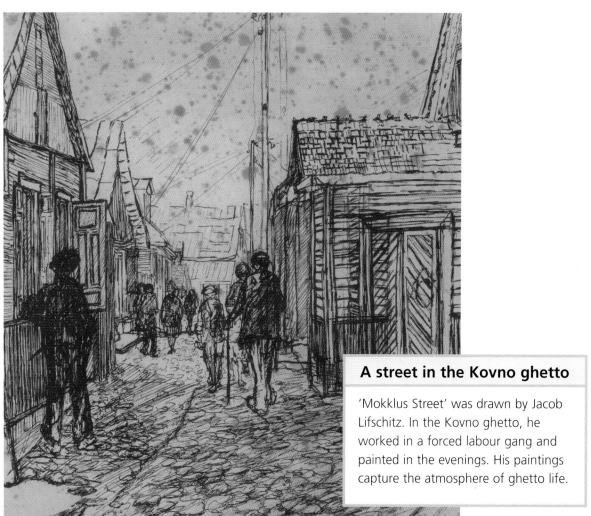

A street in the Kovno ghetto

'Mokklus Street' was drawn by Jacob Lifschitz. In the Kovno ghetto, he worked in a forced labour gang and painted in the evenings. His paintings capture the atmosphere of ghetto life.

Children of the ghettos

Within the ghettos, adults did their utmost to make sure that children were sheltered from the harsh reality of their strange and hostile world. Efforts were made to secure better living conditions and play areas for the children. Providing them with education was a high priority. Schools were set up in the Lodz ghetto during the first two years but as thousands more people arrived, schools were turned into living accommodation instead. A young boy, David Sierakowiak, kept a diary in which he wrote about his school and the quality of what he learned there:

> Sunday, April 27, 1941
> 'Today was the first day of school...
> The school is located in a tiny building which can hardly hold our benches. For now there are no other supplies (not even a blackboard). There is no cloakroom, and in the classroom we sit wearing our coats. Today we already had six classes.'

> Monday, May 26, 1941
> '...We're working now on Cicero's often-praised speech against Cataline, and next week we will start metrics. In mathematics we're doing equations. In other subjects, except German, we are falling behind.'

Children's work

This child's painting was accompanied by a rhyme:
Hurray! All their troubles are gone!
The ice is cleared, the bar undone,
the goblins their mischief cease
to frolic and romp with ease.
Shoo, shoo, sad thoughts, off you run!
Now let's happy be and have fun!

Hurray! Hurray! Hurray!

Work is fun!

This picture by Józef Kowner and the one on page 22 are examples of 18 pictures drawn for an album showing the work done by children in the Lodz ghetto. Each picture had a rhyme like the one on the previous page.

Many of them are very interesting, even if we don't remember they were painted in the ghetto. But many of them also show us the harshness of life there – some artists were determined to leave a record of their people's sufferings. Many artists died because they disobeyed the Nazis' rules about what they were allowed to draw and paint.

As the war went on, the demand for labour in the Lodz ghetto increased and children were put to work. About 700 children were educated as they worked in the underwear and dress workshop. Children also enjoyed the plays and puppet shows that were performed for them in the ghetto.

Art in the ghettos

Several internationally known Jewish artists were confined to the ghettos. Many of them were deliberately sent to the Terezín ghetto, near Prague. There they were encouraged to paint because Terezín was the centre of a huge Nazi **propaganda** exercise. Hitler made a film of this ghetto to try to show the rest of the world that he was providing a good life for the Jews (*see page 44*).

In the years since the war, paintings and drawings have provided us with images of day-to-day life in the ghettos. Some of these pictures appear on these pages.

Ghetto lullabies

Of all the poetry of the ghettos, the lullabies are the most deeply moving. Their words speak to babies and small children of their parents' hopes, fears and despair. This is a lullaby from the Lodz ghetto by Yeshayahu Szpigel:

> *Close your eyes,*
> *And the birds will come*
> *To circle around your cradle.*
> *Bundle in hand,*
> *Our house, ashes and brand,*
> *We're leaving, my child, to seek happiness.*
>
> *God has closed down the world,*
> *And all around us is night*
> *It awaits us with shuddering and fear*
> *We both stand here,*
> *In this hard, hard hour,*
> *And the path leads who knows where.*
>
> *We were chased from our home*
> *Stripped to the bone,*
> *Through the dark, driven into the field,*
> *And hail, snow and wind*
> *Accompanied you, my child,*
> *Accompanied you into the abyss of a world.*

Ghetto diaries

Many people in the ghettos wrote diaries. It is clear from their content that these were written deliberately to keep a record for future generations. The writers went to a great deal of trouble to hide their diaries in places where they would not only be safe from discovery by their guards but also where they would be preserved from damage, if necessary, for some time. People have continued to find diaries since the end of the war, some hidden away or buried in ceramic jars or in specially sealed containers.

The diaries are valuable because they tell us in detail about day-to-day life in the ghettos. They describe the hardships and the struggle of the inmates to come to terms with the cold, hunger and sickness. They record moments of happiness, as well as sadness. They show how much people clung to the hope that everything would one day be back to normal. Some are diaries written by men who were forced to make decisions about the fate of fellow Jews. Sometimes, it is clear that the pain and suffering was so great that there were almost no words to describe them.

One subject that seems to come up in nearly all the diaries is the deportations. Thousands of people from the ghettos were regularly loaded into wagons and taken away. They were often the elderly and small children. Those left behind in the ghettos were deliberately not told where their friends and relatives were being taken. Rumours spread wildly, but slowly the truth began to dawn. People realized that their fellow inmates were never coming back. The constant threat of deportations created a permanent sense of fear and apprehension.

A paper record

The diaries were written either in exercise books or often in the margins of books that had been taken into the ghetto amongst personal belongings.

16 October 1942

'The word in the street is that the "Liar" [code name for the radio] announced that only 300,000 of the 3,000,000 Polish Jews remain, and that the rest were killed in his deportations. I do not believe it, although one could believe it after watching the deportation procedure. They went out and searched only for people who were unable to work: children under the age of ten, old people over sixty years of age, the ill ... They sent away children up to age ten without parents, sent sick people from the hospitals with the one nightshirt that they'd slept in. For what? It's been said that they took them to Chelmno ... where there's a gas house where they are poisoned ...'

3 August 1944 [the end of the Lodz ghetto]

'I write these lines in a terrible state of mind – we have all of us to leave this ghetto within a few days ... Biebow, the German Ghetto-Chief, held a speech for the Jews ... He asked the crowd if they are ready to work faithfully for the Reich, and all answered "Yes". What sort of people are these Germans, that they managed to transform us into such low, crawling creatures; is life really so worthy?

When I look on my little sister, my heart is melting. Hasn't the child suffered her share? ... What will they do with our sick? with our old? with our young? ... I don't even know if I shall be allowed to be together with my sister. I cannot write more. I am more resigned terribly and black spirited.'

From the diary of Menachem Oppenheim, who was in the Lodz ghetto.

Guards at the gate

In this photograph, German and Jewish police guard one of the entrances to the Lodz ghetto. A crowd of Jewish residents has gathered in the background.

The Kovno ghetto

The Nazis thought that people would never know how they treated the victims of the Holocaust. However, Dr Elkhanan Elkes, who the Germans placed in charge of the Kovno ghetto, ordered that all its inhabitants should help keep a detailed history of the ghetto. They could take photographs, write diaries or poetry and do paintings. The response was enthusiastic. Young and old kept detailed diaries. A keen photographer, George Kadish, took many photographs at great risk to himself. Artists, such as Esther Lurie and Josef Schlesinger, drew and painted pictures. Much of this evidence was lost, but some survived because it was carefully buried or hidden. Some of these works were saved by survivors. Others lay undiscovered for many years after the war. Together, these works make sure that the memories of the appalling conditions and Nazi atrocities in the Kovno ghetto have survived for posterity.

Josef Schlesinger

Josef Schlesinger began his training at the Prague Academy of Fine Arts just before the Germans **occupied** Czechoslovakia. He went to Kovno to join his father and was confined in the ghetto after the Nazi invasion of Lithuania. There he worked in the ghetto's Paint and Sign Workshop. Here, under cover of his work, he organized secret art exhibitions. His pen and ink drawing of a particularly significant event in the ghetto – the public hanging of Nahum Meck in 1942 – was placed in the secret exhibition. Meck had been caught smuggling and had shot at a German guard. Diary entries and children's drawings show that his execution had shocked the inmates. Afterwards, Meck's mother and sister were taken to the square in Fort IX and murdered by the Nazis.

The Hanging of Meck

The Hanging of Meck, Josef Schlesinger, 1942.

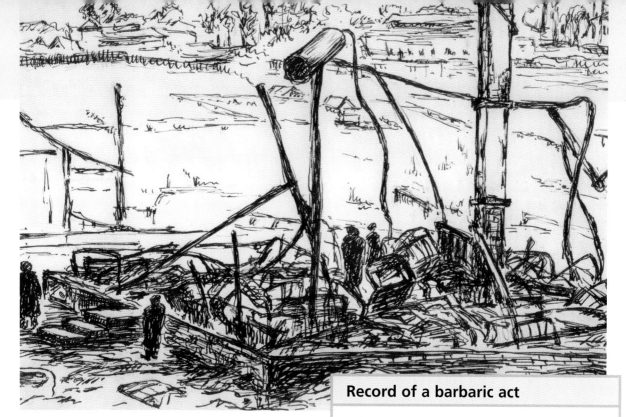

Record of a barbaric act

What Was Left of the Hospital, Esther Lurie, (undated) shows the aftermath of the burning of a hospital in the Kovno ghetto.

Esther Lurie

The Nazis in the Kovno ghetto also made use of established artists. They were ordered to paint landscapes and portraits. Sometimes they copied great masterpieces. But behind the scenes, they painted what they saw around them. Esther Lurie became very important in creating Kovno's secret **archive**. She had formal training in art and had already won prizes for her work in Tel Aviv (now in Israel), where she designed theatre sets. Unluckily, she returned to Europe late in 1938 and so was caught by the Nazis. Some of her paintings of simple landscapes actually show where dreadful atrocities took place. One area was Fort IX where brutal mass-killings regularly took place. One of the worst of these was on 29 October 1941, when 9200 inhabitants were taken to the square in the middle of the fort and murdered – 4200 of these were children.

One of Esther's pen and ink drawings records a barbaric act that happened in October 1941. It shows the charred remains of one of the ghetto's hospitals. There was an outbreak of contagious disease so Nazi officials ordered that the hospital should be burned. Orders forbade any attempt to put out the blaze. All the doctors, nurses and patients, including many children, perished in the blaze. The event is also recorded in surviving diaries. People also feared that any future outbreak would be dealt with in the same way.

Altogether, Esther Lurie produced over 200 paintings and drawings in the ghetto, but many of these were lost. Esther survived and was able to reconstruct some of her lost paintings from photographs of the originals taken at the time.

Records of resistance

Art, music and writing record people's resistance to **Nazi persecution**. There was also more violent resistance in the **ghettos**. Kovno had its own underground organization linked to Jewish **partisans** living in the forests around the ghetto. Many of these had escaped. Other ghettos also had underground organizations that planned armed uprisings. In 1943, rumours of **deportations** sparked an uprising in the Bialystok ghetto in north-eastern Poland. The same rumours were to blame for a larger uprising in the Warsaw ghetto. This began on 18 January 1943 and lasted until 16 May. It was a particularly violent uprising, partly because Jewish resistance fighters, led by Mordecai Anielewicz, openly fought the Germans. A careful record was kept of the events in diaries. These were found hidden in a milk churn after the end of the war.

The Warsaw ghetto's secret archive

In the Warsaw ghetto, historian Emanuel Ringelblum encouraged artists and writers to build up a secret **archive**. It was called *Oneg Shabbat* ('Joy of the Sabbath'). Abraham Lewin was an important contributor and kept a detailed account of the last days of the ghetto. The earliest surviving entry was for March 1942. Despite personal tragedies, he carefully recorded the terror and destruction, until 16 January 1943, when he and his daughter were probably killed. Ringelblum was also executed shortly afterwards. Lewin's diaries were part of the hidden archive, discovered after the war ended.

Inside the Warsaw ghetto

A painting by Roman Kramsztyk, *Old Jew with Children*. This was done in the Warsaw ghetto. The artist was eventually killed by the Nazis in 1942.

Self Portrait

Self Portrait by Gela Seksztajn, who lived and painted in the Warsaw ghetto. She died in Treblinka in August 1942.

From the diary of Abraham Lewin

Wednesday, 22 July 1942
'A day of turmoil, chaos and fear: the news about the expulsion of Jews is spreading like lightning through the town. Jewish Warsaw has suddenly died, the shops are closed. Jews run by, in confusion, terrified. The Jewish streets are an appalling sight – the gloom is indescribable. There are dead bodies in several places ... Beggar children are being rounded up into wagons.'

Friday, 31 July 1942
'The tenth day of the slaughter that has no parallel in our history ... They are driving the old people from the old people's home at 52 Nowolopki Street. Those rounded up are divided up into those fit for work, those able to survive and those not fit to be transported. The last group is killed on the spot.'

Wednesday, 5 August 1942
'The "action" continues unabated. We have no more strength to suffer. There are many murders. They kill the sick who don't go down to the courtyards ... Whoever falls into the hands of the Germans or the Jewish police is seized.'

Sunday, 9 August 1942
'The 19th day of the "action" of which human history has not seen the like. From yesterday the expulsion took on the character of a pogrom, or a simple massacre. They roam through the streets and murder people in their dozens, in their hundreds. Today, they are pulling endless wagons full of corpses – uncovered – through the streets.'

Friday, 21 August 1942
'Yesterday evening after six the Jewish police moved into the buildings which were supposed to have been evacuated by their occupants. They drove the occupants out by force, broke into locked flats, robbed and looted and smashed whatever they found and at the same time seized women, especially those who had no papers. Where did the Jews get this brutality from?'

Jewish partisans and their music

Resistance in the ghettos was doomed to failure, as the destruction of the Warsaw ghetto shows. Whenever possible, young men and women escaped from the ghettos to join partisan groups in the forests of Poland, Ukraine and parts of the Soviet Union. This was dangerous. They not only risked being caught, but they were also frequently rejected by the non-Jewish partisans on whom they depended for shelter and support. The situation seemed to improve from the summer of 1942, as they came to be more accepted. Family camps were established in the forests for Jewish partisans and their families, but only a small number of Jews escaped death by joining the partisans.

By this time, Jewish people were resisting the Germans by actively fighting, derailing enemy trains and blowing up bridges. From 1943, Jewish-only partisan units were formed. These were important because they helped their members to hang on to their cultural identity and the idea of belonging to one nation. Much of this happened during evening sessions around the campfire. Songs were sung to the music of the accordion, often in **Yiddish**. Sometimes, the entertainment was provided by former professional entertainers, such as a group called *Gop so smykom* ('Jump for Joy'), which performed popular songs and dances in the forest camps.

Jewish partisans

This picture shows members of a Jewish partisan unit in Byelorussia during the Second World War.

Shmerke Kaczerginski

Shmerke Kaczerginski was a poet and songwriter before the war. He lived in Vilna where he wrote songs about the struggle of the working classes. When he was imprisoned in the Vilna ghetto he continued to write songs about the Jewish struggle. His songs were very popular with the Jewish partisans. He also collected songs and poems from the ghettos to make sure that they were not forgotten. One of these was a song by Hirsh Glik, who had been inspired by the Warsaw ghetto resistance. It became the anthem of the Jewish partisans. Glik was later killed escaping from a labour camp in Estonia. He had been sent there for attempting to organize an uprising in the Vilna ghetto.

Kaczerginski later described how Hirsh Glik had inspired him when they met in the Vilna ghetto. Glik had spent some time in Warsaw and experienced the spirit of those leading the resistance to the Nazis there:

> 'The next day, Hirsh stopped by quite early. "Listen closely," he said. He sang quietly at first, but with fiery passion. His eyes were ablaze. I wondered: Where does he find such unshakeable faith? As his voice grew firmer, he began to hammer out the words, stamping his feet as if he were now on the march ... "Wonderful, Hirsh, wonderful." Through his words, I felt the impact that the Warsaw rising had made on him.'

The Jewish Partisans' Anthem
by Hirsh Glik

Never say that you have reached the final road
Though lead-grey clouds conceal blue
*   skies above,*
The hour that we've longed for now
*   draws near,*
Our steps proclaim like drumbeats:
*   We Are Here!*

From green, palmy lands and countries
*   white with snow,*
We come with all our suffering and woe;
And wherever any of our blood is shed,
Our courage and our valour rise again!

Tomorrow's sun will turn this day to gold,
And this dark night will vanish with the foe,
But should tomorrow's sun await the dawn
*   too long,*
Let this song ring out for ages yet to come!

Not with lead was this song written, but
*   with blood;*
It wasn't warbled in the forest by a bird!
But a people, trapped between collapsing walls,
With weapons held in hand – they sang
*   this song!*

So, never say that you have reached the
*   final road,*
Though lead-grey clouds conceal blue
*   skies above,*
The hour that we've longed for now
*   draws near,*
Our steps proclaim like drumbeats:
*   We Are Here!*

Camps and death camps

As soon as Hitler came to power in 1933, he established **concentration camps** in Germany. Anyone who opposed the **Nazis**, or, later, who was thought racially **inferior**, was sent there. From 1942, the Nazis carried out their '**Final Solution**' – the complete extermination of the **Jews** and other **undesirables**. This mass murder was carried out mainly in six **death camps** – Auschwitz-Birkenau, Belzec, Sobibor, Treblinka, Chelmno and Majdanek.

African Germans

Hitler regarded black people as an inferior race. A number of people of African origin had arrived in Germany at the end of the First World War. They had formed relationships with German women. The children of these mixed relationships were called mulattos. The Nazis hated them in the same way that they hated the Jews.

Many were sterilized so that they could not have children. Others were used for medical experimentation or were murdered. This policy spread across German-occupied Europe after 1939. Black prisoners of war were treated very badly in concentration camps such as Dachau and Buchenwald. Black **civilians** in Nazi Europe were put into **internment camps**. Some of these people were artists and musicians.

Josef Nassy

Josef Nassy was an African American living in Belgium. He also had a Jewish background. He was one of 2000 American passport holders who were imprisoned in an internment camp during the war. Nassy was at Laufen. Prisoners at Laufen were kept under the terms of the Geneva Convention (an international agreement protecting foreign prisoners from mistreatment). Josef was allowed to paint. During his three-year imprisonment, he produced over 200 paintings of life in Laufen.

Laufen

Josef Nassy spent the war in this camp at Laufen in Germany. As they were held under the terms of the Geneva Convention, the inmates did not have to wear prison clothes or work. However, the conditions were still bleak, as Nassy has shown.

Concentration camps

At concentration camps such as Dachau and Buchenwald, life was very different. Starvation and severe punishments were routine. The inmates were forced to do very heavy work to help the German war effort. They were literally worked to death.

Besides political prisoners, **Jehovah's Witnesses**, **homosexuals** and Jews, there were thousands of **Gypsies**. They were brutally treated but struggled to maintain their family and cultural life in the camps. Gypsy bands played their traditional music with violins and accordions, often under orders from the guards to 'welcome' prisoners back from a day of hard labour or to drown the sounds of their fellow prisoners being beaten. From 1942, Gypsies were **transported** to the death camps for extermination.

Dachau song

This song of the forced labour gangs at Dachau gives a vivid picture of life there:

Charged with death, high tension wire
Rings around our world a chain.
Pitiless a sky sends fire,
Biting frost and drenching rain.

Far from us is lust for living,
Far our women, our town,
When we mutely march to toiling
Thousands into morning's dawn.
(Refrain)
But we all learned the motto of Dachau to heed
And became as hardened as stone
Stay humane, Dachau mate,
Be a man, Dachau mate,
And work as hard as you can, Dachau mate,
For work leads to freedom alone!

Faced by ever threatening rifles,
We exist by night and day,
Life itself this hell-hole stifles
Worse than any words can say.

Days and weeks we leave unnumbered
Some forget the count of years
And their spirit is encumbered
With their faces scarred by fears.
(Refrain)
Lift the stone and drag the wagon
Shun no burden and no chore
Who you were in days long bygone
Here you are not any more.

Stab the earth and bury depthless
All the pity you can feel,
And within your own sweat, hapless
You convert to stone and steel.
(Refrain)
Once will sound the siren's wailing
Summons to the last role call
Outside then we will be hailing
Dachau mates uniting all.

Freedom brightly will be shining,
For the hard-forged brotherhood
And the work we are designing
Our work it will be good.

Auschwitz-Birkenau

The largest proportion of men, women and children who arrived at Auschwitz-Birkenau after 1942 went immediately to the **gas chambers**. Those who escaped this fate were spared to work. Many children, especially twins, were selected for medical experimentation by Joseph Mengele. For some time, Gypsies were also used for experiments until Hitler decided that they, too, should be killed like the Jews. Others who were useful to the Nazis in the camp in a variety of ways lived longer. These included artists and musicians. You have already read about Dinah Gottlieb (*see page 13*) and David Olère (*see page 5*) whose skills as artists were exploited in Auschwitz. Musicians were also given more privileges than their fellow inmates.

Dinah Gottlieb and the Gypsies

Dinah Gottlieb survived because Josef Mengele admired her work. At the time, the 13,000 Gypsies in Auschwitz were kept in a separate area of the camp. The Nazis had not yet decided whether they were an inferior race and should be killed. Mengele was studying them to identify their racial origins. Dinah was told to draw them because the photographs that had been taken of them were not clear enough for him to study their features in detail. She selected a group of Gypsies as her models. One of them was a young woman called Celine. She was Dinah's age and they became friends. Dinah deliberately painted her portrait very slowly, but once Mengele had all the detail he needed he declared that it was finished. She never saw Celine again. By this time, Hitler had decided on the fate of the Gypsies at Auschwitz. It was extermination. They all died in the gas chambers in August 1944. Dinah survived and went to live in Paris, then later, in California.

Gypsy caravan

This gypsy caravan and violin are on permanent display at the United States Holocaust Memorial Museum in Washington DC. They are a reminder that Jews were not the only victims of the Holocaust.

Fania Fenelon and Anita Lasker-Wallfisch

Fania Fenelon and Anita Lasker-Wallfisch were members of camp orchestras. When they arrived they were treated the same as everybody else – their heads were shaved and a number was tattooed on their arms. Anita tells of how she was questioned about her work before the war. When she said that she played the cello, she was separated from the rest. The conductor of the camp orchestra was the niece of the German composer Gustav Mahler. She took Anita into the orchestra. The orchestra was ordered to play as the forced labour parties were marched out of the camp each morning.

Fania Fenelon was a member of a women's orchestra in Auschwitz. She played for the camp commandant, Josef Kramer, but was also expected to play happy tunes as men, women and children were forced into the gas chambers. Both Fania and Anita survived.

Sunday concert

This photograph shows an Auschwitz Orchestra Sunday concert performed for **SS** officers at the camp.

Excerpt from *Gypsy Song* by David Beigelman

David Beigelman was a professional composer and musician in Poland before the war. He was sent to the Lodz **ghetto** where he was the musical director for the ghetto theatre. He later died in Auschwitz.

The night is dark,
as dark as ink.
With quaking heart
I think and think.
No others live in
such grief as we're given
We go unfed:
no crust of bread.

Wall paintings in Auschwitz

At Auschwitz-Birkenau **concentration camp**, some of the most interesting artwork was done by inmates on the walls. The buildings of the camp are still standing, so we can see the artwork today. Dinah Gottlieb, for example, first came to the notice of her Nazi captors after she had decorated the wall of the dormitory for children that had arrived in the camp from the Terezín **ghetto** in Czechoslovakia. The Czech prisoners used art to protect the children as much as possible from the horror of Auschwitz.

Dinah painted the story of *Snow White and the Seven Dwarfs* at the children's request. Later they performed the story.

Other wall decorations for children that can still be seen show us the skill of the artists. They also show how the inmates tried to bring beauty, dignity and colour into their lives. Stencil paintings of camels and pyramids decorate one of the barrack blocks. Cherubs, horseback riders and kittens add some kind of normality to the washrooms in another block.

Boy on a hobby horse

Adults painted pictures, like this one, on the walls of camp buildings used by children to try to make the surroundings more attractive and colourful.

The *Königsgraben* painting

At Birkenau there was a special penal company (the *Strafkompanie*). This was made up of prisoners the Nazis thought were particularly dangerous because they belonged to the camp's underground resistance movement. Others were sent there as punishment for disobeying camp rules. From May 1942 until July 1943, they were housed in a separate barrack and set to work building the *Königsgraben* (King's canal). This was extremely gruelling work, digging a drainage ditch in a swampy area of Birkenau. The prisoners were given little food and punishments were very severe. Large numbers of prisoners died. An unknown artist painted this scene of their labour on the ceiling of the barracks, where it can still be seen.

37

Reflection

The end of the war and the defeat of Germany in 1945 brought freedom – of a kind. As survivors emerged shocked and starved from the **concentration camps** and **ghettos**, their ordeal was still not over. They were homeless and penniless. They were still treated badly by their neighbours when they returned to their homes. Hundreds were also to find that they were almost completely alone in the world. To the agonizing memories of their own suffering was added the pain of discovering that their loved ones were lost forever. Many were so distressed and disturbed that it was years before they could talk about their experiences.

For the soldiers, journalists and other **civilians** who liberated the camps, the horror of what they discovered deeply affected them. The images of death, destruction and suffering would never leave them. The reality of the Holocaust was so overwhelming that they too found they could not talk about it. Many turned to art, music and poetry as a way of expressing things. For survivors, it was a means of expressing their anger, their indignation and their deep sense of loss.

Mervyn Peake

Mervyn was born in China in 1911 and returned home to England as a boy. As a young man, he gained a reputation as a painter and illustrator, then as a poet and novelist. When war broke out he went into the army. Towards the end of the war, after leaving the army, he was sent with a journalist to draw the scenes of devastation caused by the war. As a result, he was one of the first Britons to enter the concentration camp at Bergen-Belsen. This experience deeply influenced his work from that time onwards. He was also a writer and he became obsessed with the idea of the struggle against overwhelming power and destructive forces. He expressed this idea in his books, the *Gormenghast Trilogy*, especially in *Titus Alone*. The first book in the trilogy was published in 1946 and the last in 1959.

Witness of death

Gassing by David Olère. After being freed from Auschwitz, David was able to empty out on to his canvas the terrible scenes of the gas chambers that he held inside his head. His collection of paintings is entitled *The Eyes of a Witness*.

The Consumptive, Belsen 1945

Mervyn Peake went into Bergen-Belsen with British troops in 1945. He wrote this poem and made this drawing after he had witnessed scenes of sickness and suffering there:

If seeing her an hour before her last
Weak cough into all blackness I could yet
Be held by chalk-white walls, and by the great
Ash coloured bed,
And the pillows hardly creased
By the tapping of her little cough-jerked head –
If such can be a painter's ecstasy,
(Her limbs like pipes, her head a china skull)
Then where is mercy?

Music of remembrance

The aftermath of the Holocaust also inspired composers. Survivors composed some of the most moving pieces of music, using music to express their deep pain and sorrow. One such piece is called *Terezín*. It was written by a survivor of the ghetto, Karl Berman.

Other works are dedicated to those whose sufferings have become well known, for example Oskar Morawetz's *From the Diary of Anne Frank: Oratorio for Voice and Orchestra*. This is dedicated to Anne Frank and includes parts of her diary set to music. In 1947, Arnold Schoenberg, whose music had been banned by the **Nazis**, wrote *A Survivor From Warsaw*. This is a short but powerful piece based on the story of a survivor of the Warsaw ghetto. It describes the moment when the crowds showed their defiance when faced with death by singing a traditional Jewish song, *Shema Israel* ('Hear, O Israel'). The words are from the Old Testament of the Bible.

In 1962, Russian composer Dmitri Shostakovich composed *Babi Yar* to commemorate the slaughter of 70,000 Ukrainian Jews at a ravine on the outskirts of Kiev. This work, inspired by the Holocaust, is important because it is the first statement against **anti-Semitism** in the history of Russian music. In 1968, the American composer Charles Davidson set many of the poems of the children of Terezín to music. This song cycle is called *I Never Saw Another Butterfly*.

Words of remembrance

It took years for many of the survivors of the Holocaust to speak out about their experiences. At the trial of Adolf Eichmann, who sent thousands of Hungarian Jews to the **gas chambers**, many survivors gave evidence about the terrible things they had seen and endured. Since the trial, the **archives** of oral and written evidence of the Holocaust have grown into a lasting memorial. Artists and writers continue to be drawn to the subject.

Nelly Sachs

Nelly was born in Berlin in 1891. She began writing romantic poems at the age of seventeen. Her first book, a collection of historical tales, was published in 1921. However, the Holocaust changed her work dramatically. Her friendship with a Swedish writer saved her life, as she and her mother were able to leave Nazi Germany. During the war, her poetry became dominated by the cruelty and atrocities experienced by Jews. Her first two volumes of these poems were published in 1947 and 1949. Her work throughout her life continued to reflect her obsession with the suffering of the Holocaust. She received the Nobel Prize for Literature in 1966 and died in Sweden in 1970.

Elie Wiesel

Elie Wiesel was Hungarian. The Wiesel family was taken to Auschwitz in 1942. His mother and younger sister died immediately in the gas chambers.

If Only I Knew by Nelly Sachs

If only I knew
On what your last look rested.
Was it a stone that had drunk
So many last looks that they fell
Blindly upon its blindness?

Or was it earth,
Enough to fill a shoe,
And black already
With so much parting
And with so much killing?

Or was it your last road
That brought you a farewell from all
*   the roads*
You had walked?

A puddle, a bit of shining metal,
Perhaps the buckle of an enemy's belt,
Or some small augury
Of heaven?

Or did this earth,
Which lets no one depart unloved,
Send you a bird-sign through the air,
Reminding your soul that it quivered
In torment of its burnt body.

Elie, his father and two older sisters were selected for work. He and his father were sent to Buchenwald, where his father died. After he was freed, Wiesel became a respected academic. His writing has been completely devoted to making sure people know the truth about the victims of the Holocaust, because he was there and he shared their suffering.

Never Shall I Forget by Elie Wiesel

Never shall I forget that night,
the first night in the camp
which has turned my life into one
*   long night,*
seven times cursed and seven times sealed.

Never shall I forget that smoke,
Never shall I forget the little faces of
*   the children*
whose bodies I saw turned into wreaths
*   of smoke*
beneath a silent blue sky.

Never shall I forget those flames
which consumed my faith for ever.
Never shall I forget that nocturnal silence
which deprived me for all eternity of the
*   desire to live.*

Never shall I forget those moments
which murdered my God and my soul
and turned my dreams to dust.

Never shall I forget these things,
even if I am condemned to live
as long as God Himself.

Never.

Memorials

Some of the artistic work inspired by the Holocaust since 1945 can be seen in memorials. This one in Warsaw was erected in 1948 to commemorate the brave resistance of the inhabitants of the Warsaw ghetto.

Never forget

The Holocaust was a human tragedy on an unimaginable scale. The paintings, diaries, letters and poems that survive from the time are extremely important because they help us to recognize that those who suffered and died were human beings – young and old. They had fears, anxieties and moments of joy, just like us. Their only 'crime' was that their culture or religion made them different.

The Terezín ghetto

The *Theresienstadt* (Terezín) was originally a military fort about 60 kilometres (37 miles) from Prague (now in the Czech Republic). From 1941, Czech **Jews** were forced to leave their homes to live there. Soon, hundreds arrived from all over eastern Europe. The overcrowded conditions were as harsh and cruel as in other **ghettos**. However, Terezín ghetto is remembered for its rich cultural life – the beautiful poetry and painting of its children and the amazing creativity of its artists, composers and musicians. Hitler recognized how this could be used for **propaganda**. He showed Terezín to the world as a model settlement where Jews could live and flourish safe from **persecution**. He even opened it up for **Red Cross** visitors so that they could see for themselves what was happening there.

The creativity of the children of Terezín

About 15,000 children passed through Terezín ghetto between 1941 and 1944, but only about 100 survived the war. Most of them died in Auschwitz. They are remembered by the collection of around 4000 pictures and hundreds of poems that they left behind. Although the children suffered cruelty, disease and starvation, they were sheltered from the reality of their surroundings as much as possible. They were still educated. They were encouraged to write and draw. With the help of Friedl Dicker-Brandeis, an artist, they created a bright and colourful world in their paintings. However, their poems show us a deeper fear and longing. It is very sad for us today to read how they hoped that they would one day return to their homes, towns and villages and be reunited with their families, when we know what really happened.

The Butterfly

The last, the very last,
So richly, brightly, dazzlingly yellow.
Perhaps if the sun's tears would sing
Against a white stone.

Such, such a yellow
Is carried lightly way up high.
It went away I'm sure because it wished to kiss the world good-bye.

For seven weeks I've lived in here,
Penned up inside this ghetto.
But I have found what I love here,
The dandelions call to me
And the white chestnut branches in
*   the court.*
Only I never saw another butterfly.

That butterfly was the last one.
Butterflies don't live here,
in the ghetto.

This poem was written by Pavel Friedmann, who died in Auschwitz in 1944.

Vedem ('In the Lead')

One group of teenage boys produced a carefully handwritten and amazingly creative secret magazine. It was done without the help of adults in a concealed area in their barracks known to them as the 'Republic of Shkid'. Their magazine contained articles, poems and drawings. When the boys were eventually sent to Auschwitz, the magazine was saved by one of the survivors.

Extract from an article in Vedem, Terezín, 1943

In this extract from Vedem, Petr Ginz describes his task of bringing food from the kitchens to the hospital:

'An Unsuccessful Ramble Through Terezín

At last we set out. The journey was uneventful and we reached the Hamburg barracks, where the dietary kitchen is now situated, without mishap. Recalling my newspaper duties, I tried to get some sort of interview going.

- How many people does this kitchen serve?
- Why do you ask?
- If you want to know, I am the editor of a magazine called Vedem.
- That's a good one – an editor – ho, ho, ho. Well, if you must know, about 450. That kind of conversation was not to my taste and so I took the container of mashed potatoes and left ... Oh what pen could describe our sufferings on this arduous pilgrimage! The wind drove sand into our faces, soup spilled from our buckets over our coats and into our shoes... Kališek was pleased. His feet were warm, he said, because hot soup was slushing about in his shoes.'

Music and theatre in Terezín

Between 1941 and 1945, the theatre flourished in Terezín. All sort of plays, cabarets, puppet shows and concerts were performed, all staged with scenery and costumes. This was partly due to the large number of artists and musicians who were sent there. Fourteen operas were performed, including *The Marriage of Figaro, Tosca* and *Cavalleria Rusticana*. This was thanks to the work of Rafael Schechter, a talented pianist and composer. He established a choir in Terezín soon after his arrival in 1941. Schechter and his choir of 150 people were later **transported** to Auschwitz where they died.

Brundibar

This copy of an old photograph shows the final scene from the opera *Brundibar* as it appeared in the propaganda film made by the Nazis in 1944.

Hans Krása and *Brundibar*

Hans Krása was born in Prague in 1899. By the time he was eleven, his first musical composition had been performed in public. He studied music at the German Academy of Music in Prague. He led a fashionable life, mixing with writers, artists and poets. In Terezín he composed several pieces. His best-known work was the children's opera, *Brundibar*, which was not only performed in the ghetto but which was also filmed by the **Nazis** for propaganda purposes. They wanted the world to believe that the inmates were being treated properly.

The opera was first performed on 23 October 1943. It is the story of two needy people who the local children decide to help by holding a street collection. Suddenly, Brundibar, an evil organ grinder appears and takes all the money they have collected. Children played the parts of the birds and animals who make sure that Brundibar returns the money he has stolen. *Brundibar* was performed 55 times. In spite of his talent and success, Hans Krása was sent to Auschwitz where he died in the **gas chambers** on 17 October 1944. He composed what was to be his final work only four days before leaving Terezín.

The puppet theatre

It is amazing that, in spite of living in such awful conditions, people could still make puppets, scenery and lighting effects. Twenty-two puppet shows were performed in Terezín to the delight of the small children in the ghetto.

Victor Ullmann, Petr Kien and the *Emperor of Atlantis*

Victor Ullmann was a student of the composer Arnold Schoenberg in Vienna. He was a totally dedicated and hard-working musician. Like Hans Krása, he composed a huge number of pieces, and continued to write after he had been sent to Terezín. Petr Kien wrote words to go with the music, and, together with Ullman, produced the opera *Emperor of Atlantis*.

In fact, Kien wrote two versions. One was handwritten and the second was typed. The first was fiercely critical of Hitler and the Nazis. The second, much milder version was shown to the camp officials to make sure they would be allowed to perform the opera. On the surface it appears to be a simple story, but the underlying theme is the horror of the **concentration camps**. The main characters are the Emperor, the Loudspeaker, the Drummer-girl and Death. The Emperor is Hitler, the Loudspeaker is Goebbels and the Drummer-girl is Hitler's deputy, Herman Goering. The other characters – the soldier and the young girl – are caught up in the horror of war. In the story, Death goes on strike because he is unable to cope with the devastating effects of war and hunger. Without the help of Death, the Emperor cannot rule. Instead, Death supports the ordinary human beings until the Emperor (Hitler) accepts his own death. This version of the opera was not performed until after the war was over!

Drama

Plays were also performed in Terezín. This was mainly as a result of the work of Gustav Schorsch, who had studied drama in Prague. He was in charge of the theatre section in Terezín. His productions included *Measure for Measure* by William Shakespeare.

The artists of Terezín

The real world of Terezín was captured by a group of talented painters. The Nazis labelled their work 'horror propaganda'. In fact, their paintings portrayed the truth about life in Terezín. The artists were questioned and tortured. Almost all of them died as a result.

Leo Haas

Leo Haas was one of the survivors of the Holocaust. He had studied at the Berlin Art Academy and worked in Vienna before returning to Czechoslovakia. He was deported to Terezín in December 1942. Here, under the cover of working in the Drawing Office of the Technical Department (where artists were used by the Nazis to draw plans for them), he painted and drew the reality of life at Terezín. He was arrested in 1944, imprisoned and later moved to other camps until he was set free at the end of the war. He had a distinguished career after the war, which included being a professor at the Art Academy of Berlin.

Fritz Taussig

Fritz Taussig was known as 'Fritta', the name he used on his paintings. Until 1941, he was a cartoonist and graphic artist in Prague. In Terezín, he was put in charge of the Technical Department and had the job of providing the Germans with drawings and plans. Like Leo Haas, he used his position to do undercover, secret artwork. Unfortunately, in July 1944, some of his work was discovered along with that of others. The artists were sent to Auschwitz. Fritta died there. His wife died in prison in Terezín. Their three-year-old son, Tommy, was adopted by Leo Haas after the war.

Art as a record

Scenes of Life in the Ghetto by Leo Haas is an example of how some artists used art to record what conditions were really like in the ghetto.

To není pohádka – to je pravda!

Tommy's book

Fritta's son Thomas was the first baby to be born in the ghetto. In fact, Jewish women were not allowed to have babies. If they became pregnant they were given **abortions** free of charge. But it was sometimes possible to hide the babies when they were born. This meant that Tommy's early years were far from those of a normal toddler. In an attempt to make up for this, Fritta produced a very touching book of drawings to celebrate his son's third birthday. The delightful illustrations in the book show Tommy's birthday celebrations as they should have been in a normal world. They are very different to the 'secret drawings' that his father drew of his real surroundings. The birthday album was hidden and discovered after the war. It was later published by the Yad Vashem memorial museum in Israel.

Pavel Fantel

Pavel Fantel was not a professional artist, but he was inspired by the hardships he endured to express himself through art. Pavel was born in Prague. He trained and then became a doctor in the Czech army. He arrived at Terezín in 1942 and worked in the hospital there. During this time, he secretly drew a series of pictures that gave

Real life or a fairy tale?

This picture from Tommy's book shows Tommy running about in a landscape filled with sunshine, butterflies and flowers. The caption reads 'This is not a fairy tale – it's real'.

a cynical view of life at Terezín. In one of these, called *Metamorphosis*, Fantel shows how an inmate of Terezín changed as a result of being imprisoned for four years in the ghetto. It is made up of a series of four pictures. In the first, the man looks plump and well fed. By the time the fourth picture is reached, he is almost a skeleton.

The history of the Terezín ghetto and its prisoners brings home to us very clearly just how much talent was lost by the destruction of life in the Holocaust. It is particularly sad that so many of the talented artists and musicians that were killed were children and young people.

The Terezín diary of Gonda Redlich

Gonda Redlich's diary was discovered in 1967 but only published completely in English in 1992. The original was written in **Hebrew**. It is in two parts. The first is a list of events in Terezín from 1942 until 1944. The second is a diary written for his baby son, Dan, after his birth on 16th March 1944.

Gonda was born in Olmütz, Moravia in 1916. When the Nazis took over Czechoslovakia in 1939, he was studying to be a lawyer. In the ghetto, Redlich was on the committee ordered by the Germans to provide lists of men, women and children to be transported.

At the beginning, no one had any idea what was happening to them. Gonda's diary, however, records his own observations of his surroundings. It talks about his hopes and fears and the awful responsibility of his official position. Occasionally, there is humour. It also confirms the reality of life in Terezín shown, for example, by the artists.

Extracts from Gonda Redlich's diary

January 4–6, 1942
'In the evening, I heard a terrible piece of news. A transport will go from Terezín to Riga (Latvia). We argued for a long while if the time had not yet come to say "enough". Our mood is very bad. We prepared for the transport. We worked practically all night. With Fredy's help, we managed to spare the children from the transport.'

January 8, 1942
'The Germans ordered the construction of gallows. All the people that sent letters are expected to be in grave danger. Haven't we reached the limit? Yet we still argue among ourselves concerning our living quarters. When I think about it, all of this is insignificant compared to the fact that it is possible some Jews may die whose only crime has been the writing of a letter to their relatives.'

January 21, 1942
'Moments of satisfaction. The woman director of the youth office conducted me to a room where they were celebrating the birthday of a small child. The other children sang songs. The sun came out and warmed the room and I almost forgot all the difficulties of our situation.'

A child of the ghetto

Charlotte Buresova's paintings were painted in such a way as to deliberately emphasize the things of beauty amongst the poverty and sorrow of the ghetto.

'Diary of Dan'

On 16 March 1944, Gonda's son, Daniel was born. At this point, he began to write a second diary. This was so that he could keep a record of his son's early years that one day they could look back upon together. The entries in the diary record special moments in Dan's young life and reveal the delight of a father in his baby son:

March 22nd 1944
'After you were born, he (the head of the Jewish community) announced your name: Dan Peter Beck, along with thirty dead and another outbreak of **typhus**. You carried your mother's family name because our marriage was performed in the ghetto and such marriages were not legal according to the law of the land.'

April 13th 1944
'Today we went out with you for the first time. We have a nice baby carriage, a product of the ghetto. Usually the craftsmanship in the ghetto is second rate, but this baby carriage is very pretty ...

'Bright afternoons. In the city square, the Jewish orchestra played. A Jewish orchestra, as if a hard war full of blood was not being fought, a war of survival.'

July 20th 1944
'Your eyes are as blue as heaven. This is no poetic exaggeration. Your eyes stand out the most. Everyone praises them ... I wanted to give your mother a gift on her birthday: a picture of you. I asked an artist to draw your picture. Today they arrested the artist, and took him to an unknown place.'

October 6th 1944 [the last entry]
'Tomorrow, we travel my son. We will travel on a transport like thousands before us ... Hopefully, the time of our redemption is near.'

Gonda, his wife and baby did not return from that last journey. They died in Auschwitz-Birkenau.

Timeline

1933

30 January	Hitler and the Nazi Party come to power in Germany
28 February	Decree is signed allowing for the creation of concentration camps to hold political opponents of the Nazis
21 March	Dachau, the first concentration camp, is established
1 April	Campaign to encourage people to boycott Jewish businesses is begun
7 April	Jews employed by the government lose their jobs
10 May	Books classified as 'degenerate' are taken from libraries all over Berlin and publicly burned

1934

5 March	Jewish actors banned from performing
7 June	Jewish students banned from taking examinations

1935

15 September	The Nuremberg Laws remove all rights and freedom from Jews and make them the focus of humiliation and discrimination

1936

	A decree is issued that says Jewish doctors and dentists are not allowed to work in state hospitals. Jews cannot become judges, join the military or work in the book trade.

1937

	Exhibition of 'Degenerate' Art is held in Munich. This includes works by Van Gogh, Matisse and Cézanne and attracts 2 million visitors.

1938

9 November	*Kristallnacht* (Night of Broken Glass). Jewish synagogues are burned and shop windows smashed. Hundreds of Jewish men are arrested and sent to concentration camps.

1939

1 September	Germany invades Poland
3 September	Second World War begins when Britain and France declare war on Germany

1940

	German and Austrian Jews attempt to find refuge in other countries. The majority are refused entry.
February	First Jews are deported from Germany to ghettos in Poland
30 April	The Lodz ghetto, in Poland, is established.

1941

	The Terezín ghetto is established outside Prague, Czechoslovakia
	The Kovno ghetto, in Lithuania, is established
June	In eastern Europe and the Soviet Union, mobile killing squads begin the mass slaughter of Jews and Gypsies

1942

20 January

The Wannsee Conference, attended by leading Nazis, takes place near Berlin. At this, the 'Final Solution' of the 'Jewish problem' is decided.

The boys of the Terezín ghetto begin producing their secret magazine, *Vedem*.

Gonda Redlich begins writing his diary in the Terezín ghetto

26 March
Deportations to Auschwitz from ghettos and camps in Europe begin

1943

January–May
Resistance in the Warsaw ghetto crushed by SS forces

David Olère deported to Auschwitz

Jewish partisan units formed in the forests of Poland and Lithuania

Children's opera, *Brundibar*, performed in the Terezín ghetto

1944

6 June
D-Day Landings in Normandy, France; the liberation of northern Europe begins

Felix Nussbaum and his family, Gonda Redlich, his wife and baby son Dan, and Petr Ginz all die in Auschwitz

1945

27 January
Soviet forces liberate Auschwitz. David Olère and Dinah Gottlieb are survivors.

11 April
Buchenwald concentration camp is liberated. Elie Weisel is a survivor.

15 April
British forces liberate Bergen-Belsen. Mervyn Peake is among the first Britons to witness the horror of the Holocaust.

7 May
Germany surrenders. The war in Europe is over.

Camps and ghettos such as Lodz, Kovno and Terezín are liberated

20 May
The Nuremberg Trials of Nazi war criminals begin. They last until October 1946.

1947

Arnold Schoenberg composes A *Survivor From Warsaw* in memory of those who died in the heroic resistance to the Nazis

Nelly Sachs' first poetry anthology is published, dedicated to Holocaust victims

1948

14 May
The creation of the Jewish state of Israel is announced. Survivors begin to emigrate there. The Jewish homeland is created at great cost to the Palestinian Arabs who live there. Other survivors seek new lives in places such as the USA, Canada, Britain, Australia and New Zealand.

1962

May
Execution of Adolf Eichmann

Dmitri Shostakovich composes *Babi Yar* in memory of the 70,000 Jews and Gypsies who were slaughtered on the outskirts of Kiev

1968

Charles Davidson sets the poems of the young people of the Terezín ghetto to music, entitled *I Never Saw Another Butterfly*

2000

Britain, the USA and some other countries in Europe observe a national Holocaust Memorial days for the first time. The art, writing and music of those who died and those who survived are moving features in these ceremonies.

Glossary

abortion medical operation carried out to end a pregnancy

anti-Semitism prejudice or hostility towards Jews

archive collection of documents and records

Aryan used by the Nazis to mean people with northern European ancestors, without any ancestors from what they called 'inferior races', such as Poles, Slavs or Jews. Aryans were supposed to be blonde, blue-eyed and sturdy.

boycott refusal to buy goods from a country, an individual or group of people

capitulation surrender, or to give up resisting something

civilian person who is not serving in the military forces of a country

communists people who believe that property should belong to the state and that each person should only be paid what they need

concentration camps camps in which those who were critical of or opposed Nazi rule were imprisoned. *See also* death camps.

crematoria special ovens designed and built to cremate (burn) bodies

death camps prison camps designed for the purpose of carrying out mass executions

degenerate corrupt or immoral

democracy system of government in which a country's citizens vote for their leaders

deportation the selection and transportation of people (deportees) from the ghettos and concentration camps to the death camps for execution

depression economic crisis usually resulting in high unemployment

dictator ruler of a state who takes total power and holds on to it by removing opposition

Einsatzgruppen special mobile forces set up to murder Jews in occupied countries

emaciated thin and weak from hunger

euthanasia programme Nazi programme of 'mercy killing' of the mentally and physically handicapped to preserve the 'purity' of the Aryan race

'Final Solution' term used to describe the plan to systematically wipe out Jews and all racial groups who did not fit into the Nazis' ideal of a pure Aryan race. The plan was discussed at the Wannsee Conference in 1942. It was to be carried out in specially equipped camps using a poisonous gas called Zyklon B.

gas chambers special buildings constructed by the Nazis at concentration camps, in which prisoners were murdered using poisonous gas

ghetto separate part of a city or town, often a slum area, where a minority group of people lived, or were forced to live

Gypsies travelling people who speak the Romany language; the Nazis called any travelling people, or those whose ancestors had been travellers, gypsies

Hebrews Jews who lived in Palestine in ancient times. Hebrew was their language, and a modern version of the language is used in the present-day state of Israel.

homosexual person who is attracted to other people of the same sex

immigration moving from one country to another

inferior not as good as someone or something else

internment camp camp set up to remove from society people whom the government thought to be undesirable

Jehovah's Witnesses a religious group

Jew someone who is a member of the Jewish religion, called 'Judaism'. The Nazis also called people Jews if they had Jewish ancestors, even if they had changed their faith.

Nazi short for *Nationalsozialistische Deutsche Arbeitpartei*: the National Socialist German Workers Party

Nazi Youth organization of young German boys started by the Nazis to make sure that Nazi ideas and beliefs were passed on to young people

occupation when one country invades and rules over another country

partisans resistance fighters in occupied countries who used techniques such as ambushes to drive the Germans out of their country

persecution being treated very badly over a period of time

pogrom organized persecution of a group whose culture and religion are different

propaganda clever advertising or public speeches and displays that have the power to influence the way people think. Joseph Goebbels was Hitler's Minister for Propaganda from 1933 to 1945.

prosperity the wealth or good fortune necessary to live a comfortable life

Red Cross non-political international organization set up to provide assistance to victims of war and natural disasters

Reichstag German parliament

Slavs groups of people native to parts of Russia, Poland and the former Czechoslovakia

Sonderkommandos special groups of prisoners in the death camps, many of them Jews, who took the bodies from the gas chambers to the crematoria

SS short for '*Schutzstaffel*' – security staff. The SS began as Hitler's personal guard. Later, some ran concentration camps and death camps. All the SS swore loyalty to Hitler personally, not to Germany.

transportations the transportations (also known as transports or deportations) were the huge convoys of several thousand people taken from the ghettos and concentration camps to the death camps, such as Auschwitz

typhus an infectious disease

undesirables people in Nazi Germany (and other parts of Europe after 1939) that the Nazis believed to be racially inferior

visa pass or certificate allowing a person to enter a foreign country

Yiddish language spoken by Jews in central and eastern Europe. It is a mixture of German dialect containing Hebrew words and those of other modern languages.

Further reading

Auschwitz, Jane Shuter (Heinemann Library, 1999)

Diary of a Young Girl, Anne Frank (Penguin, 1997)

I Never Saw Another Butterfly: Children's Drawings and Poems from Terezín Concentration Camp, 1942–1944, edited by Hana Volavkova (Schocken Books, 1993)

Ten Thousand Children: True Stories Told by Children Who Escaped the Holocaust on the Kindertransport, Anne L. Fox and Eva Abraham-Podietz (Behrman House, 1997)

The Beautiful Days of My Youth, Ana Novac (Henry Holt, 1992)

The Cap, or The Price of a Life, Roman Frister (Weidenfeld & Nicolson, 1999)

The Past is Myself, Christabel Bielenberg (Chatto and Windus, 1984)

Sources

The author and Publishers gratefully acknowledge the publications from which written sources in the book are drawn. In some cases the wording or sentence structure has been simplified to make the material appropriate for a school readership.

A Cup of Tears, Robert and Michael Lewin (Blackwell Publishers, 1989) p. 29

Anne Frank's Diary (Guild Publishing, 1980) p. 16

Art from the Ashes: A Holocaust Anthology, edited by Lawrence L. Langer (Oxford University Press, 1995) pp. 29, 40

Dachau Song (reproduced courtesy of the US Holocaust Memorial Museum) p. 33

Holocaust Poetry, compiled by Hilda Schiff (St Martin's Press, 1996) pp. 15, 41

I Have Not Seen a Butterfly Around Here: Children's Drawings and Poems from Terezín (Jewish Museum Prague) p. 42

O' The Chimneys, Nelly Sachs (Translation copyright © 1967, renewed 1995 by Farrar, Straus and Giroux, Inc. 'If Only I Knew' reprinted by permission of Farrar, Straus and Giroux, LLC) p. 40

Rise Up and Fight (a CD produced by the US Holocaust Memorial Museum, Washington DC, USA) p. 31

The Glassblowers, Mervyn Peake (Eyre & Spottiswoode, 1950. 'The Consumptive' reproduced courtesy of Methuen) p. 39

The Holocaust Exhibition website of the Imperial War Museum (http://www.iwm.org.uk/lambeth/holoc-ex1.htm) p. 39

The Last Ghetto, edited by Michel Unger (Yad Vashem Publications) pp. 22, 23

The Last Lullaby: Poetry from the Holocaust, translated by Aaron Kramer (Syracuse University Press, 1999) pp. 19, 21, 35

The Terezín Diary of Gonda Redlich, edited by Saul S. Friedman (University of Kentucky Press, 1999) pp. 48–49

Voyage of the St Louis, an online exhibition by the US Holocaust Memorial Museum (http://www.ushmm.com/stlouis/) p. 17

We Are Children Just the Same: Vedem, the Secret Magazine by the Boys of Terezín, edited by Marie Rut Krizkova (Jewish Publication Society, 1995) p. 43

Places of interest and websites

Museums and exhibitions
Imperial War Museum
Lambeth Road, London SE16 6HZ
Tel: 020 7416 5320
Website: *http://www.iwm.org.uk*
The Imperial War Museum in London now has a permanent Holocaust exhibition.

London Jewish Museum
Raymond Burton House, 129–131 Albert Street, London NW1 7NB
Tel: 020 7284 1997
Website: *http://www.jewishmuseum.org.uk*

Or:

The Sternberg Centre, 80 East End Road, London N3 2SY
Tel: 020 8349 1143
The London Jewish Museum regularly features exhibitions and talks about the Holocaust.

Sydney Jewish Museum
146 Darlinghurst Road, Darlinghurst, NSW 2010
Tel: (02) 9360 7999
Website: *http://www.sydneyjewishmuseum.com.au*
The Sydney Jewish Museum contains a permanent Holocaust exhibition, using survivors of the Holocaust as guides.

Websites
Before consulting any websites you need to know:

1 Almost all Holocaust websites have been designed for adult users. They can contain horrifying and upsetting information and pictures.
2 Some people wish to minimize the Holocaust, or even deny that it happened at all. Some of their websites pretend to be delivering unbiased facts and information. To be sure of getting accurate information it is always better to use an officially recognized site such as the ones listed below.

www.ushmm.org
This is the US Holocaust Memorial Museum site.

www.iwm.org.uk
The Imperial War Museum site. You can access Holocaust material from the main page.

www.holocaust-history.org
This is the Holocaust History Project site.

www.auschwitz.dk
The Holocaust: Crimes, Heroes and Villains site.

http://motlc.wiesenthal.com
The Museum of Tolerance's Multimedia Learning Centre site.

Index